# Stories Jesus Told

## DANIEL FUSCO

Lifeway Press®
Nashville, Tennessee

## Prodution Team

Susan Hill
*Writer*

Jennifer Siao
*Production Editor*

Reid Patton
*Content Editor*

Jon Rodda
*Art Director*

Ben Borman
*Cover Design*

Joel Polk
*Manager, Short-Term Discipleship*

Brian Daniel
*Director, Lifeway Adult Ministry*

Published by Lifeway Press® • © 2021 Daniel Fusco

ISBN 978-1-0877-3727-0 • Item 005830387

Dewey decimal classification: 226.8
Subject headings: BIBLE—PARABLES / JESUS CHRIST—PARABLES / JESUS CHRIST—TEACHINGS

Scripture taken from the New King James Version®. Copyright © 1982 by Thomas Nelson. Used by permission. All rights reserved.

To order additional copies of this resource, write to Lifeway Resources Customer Service; One Lifeway Plaza; Nashville, TN 37234; fax 615-251-5933; phone toll free 800-458-2772; order online at Lifeway.com; or email orderentry@lifeway.com.

*Printed in the United States of America*

Adult Ministry Publishing • Lifeway Resources
One Lifeway Plaza • Nashville, TN 37234

# Contents

# ABOUT THE AUTHOR

I came to a saving knowledge of Jesus Christ in 1998 while I was in my last year at Rutgers University in New Brunswick, NJ. After spending a few years touring as a professional upright and electric bass player, I felt called to pastoral ministry. My spiritual leaders confirmed this call, and I was taken on staff at Calvary Chapel Marin under the direction of Pastor John Henry Corcoran in January of 2000.

After being ordained in 2002, I was sent back to the East Coast to plant Calvary Chapel New Brunswick. In November of 2006, I turned over the church to a pastor who I had helped raise up, so I could move back to the San Francisco Bay area and plant more churches.

While I was there, I planted Calvary North Bay in Mill Valley, CA and in 2010 while continuing to pastor Calvary North Bay, I planted Calvary San Francisco. Both churches grew and I helped raise up leadership teams in each of them. I founded the Calvary Church Planting Network, which helps facilitate and support church planters.

I employ what some describe as a unique style of teaching. I like to take the timeless truths of Scripture and make them easily accessible and applicable for men and women of all ages, backgrounds, and cultures. You can find my teachings at my website, DanielFusco.com, or on iTunes, YouTube channels, and at Crossroadschurch.net. Many people start their day with my #2MinuteMessage on

my Facebook page. I also get to host the Real with Daniel Fusco TV show and the Jesus is Real Radio Ministry, featuring messages on TV and radio stations across the country.

I love to write. I'm a featured contributor to "Preaching Today," and I have published articles with Leadership Journal, pastors.com, and Calvarychapel.com. I have written four books, *Ahead of the Curve* (self-published), *Honestly: Getting Real About Jesus and Our Messy Lives* (NavPress) *Upward, Inward, and Outward: Love God, Love Yourself, Love Others* (NavPress), and *Crazy Happy: Nine Surprising Ways to Live the Truly Beautiful Life* (Waterbrook Multnomah). All books are available at Amazon.com.

I have taught at churches, retreats, youth rallies, leadership seminars, seminaries, college campuses, and pastor's conferences both in the States and abroad.

I am blessed to be married to Lynn. We live with our three children in Southwest Washington.

In 2012, God blew my mind when he led me to turn over both of those churches and move to the beautiful Pacific Northwest, where I became the Lead Pastor of Crossroads Community Church. Crossroads was one of the first mega-churches in the Northwest, founded in 1975, and God is still doing an amazing work in Vancouver/Portland area through the Crossroads family of faith.

# Stories Jesus Told

## HOW TO USE THIS STUDY

*Stories Jesus Told: Exploring the Heart of the Parables* provides a guided process for individuals and small groups to walk through the parables of Jesus. This Bible study book includes six weeks of content, each divided into two major sections: "Group Study," and "Personal Study." A leader guide is also provided to prepare those who are leading groups through this journey.

Regardless of the day of the week your group meets, each week of content begins with a group session. This group session is designed to last sixty minutes, with approximately fifteen minutes dedicated to video teaching and another forty-five minutes for group discussion. Meeting even longer than sixty minutes will allow more time for participants to interact with one another.

Each group study uses the following format to facilitate simple yet meaningful interaction among group members, with God's Word, and with the video teaching.

**Start**    This section includes questions to get the conversation started, a review of the previous week's study to reinforce the content, and an introduction to the new content for the current week.

**Watch**    This section includes key points from the video teaching, along with space for taking notes as participants watch the video.

**Discuss**    This section includes discussion questions that guide the group to respond to the video teaching and to relevant Bible passages. A second page has been provided to take notes and write down prayer requests.

Three personal studies are provided each week to take individuals deeper into Scripture and to supplement the content introduced in the group study. With biblical teaching and interactive questions, these sections challenge individuals to grow in their understanding of God's Word and to make practical application to their lives. Each week is also accompanied with a suggested Bible-reading plan to enhance the week's learning.

On pages 92-108 at the back of this book, you'll find a leader guide that will help you prepare each week. Use this guide to gain a broad understanding of the content for each week and to learn ways you can engage with members at different levels of life-changing discussion.

# SESSION 1
# Why Parables?

# GROUP STUDY

## Start

*Welcome everyone to session 1.*
*Use this page to begin the group session.*

*Begin by taking a few minutes to get to know one another.*
*Ask members of the group to introduce themselves by sharing*
*their names and how they got connected to this group study.*

**What kind of stories do you like? Fiction, non-fiction, dramas, comedy?**

**Share a book or movie that had an impact on you.**

Human beings love stories. As children, our parents and teachers read stories to us as we listened attentively. As we get older, our taste in stories matures, but we never outgrow our love for them. We wait with anticipation for new movies and new releases from our favorite authors—all because we love great stories. Jesus was a master-teacher. He knew the power of a story, so it's not surprising Jesus used stories to communicate spiritual truths. For the next six sessions, we'll be studying parables—the Stories Jesus Told.

*Pray and ask God to use your time together.*
*After praying, watch the video teaching.*

Video sessions available at lifeway.com/stories

# Watch

*Use the space below to take notes
while you watch video session 1.*

To access the teaching sessions,
use the instructions in the back
of your Bible study book.

# Discuss

Jesus was a master-teacher, who made the truths of God simple enough for anyone to understand. To encounter the stories Jesus told, we must read our Bibles. The Bible is the primary way God speaks to His people and so getting the most out of our Bible reading is an important aspect of hearing from God.

*Read Matthew 13:10-13 together.*

1.  We all want God to speak to us personally, but God has spoken to us through His Word. How would you describe your experience reading God's Word? How would you like to grow as a student of God's Word?

2.  Read Psalm 19:7-9. How does the psalmist describe God's Word? Why should this make us want to read it?

3.  Jesus used parables to keep people with closed hearts from understanding His message. What does this teach us about our posture as we approach God's Word?

4.  Why should prayer and Bible reading go hand in hand? How has prayer shaped your Bible reading?

5.  If you haven't yet, what steps can you take to make Bible reading a part of your daily routine?

6.  What do you hope to learn through the next six weeks of Bible study?

*Close your discussion with prayer. Remind those in your group to complete the personal studies and Bible reading over the next week.*

# Reading Plan

*Over the next week, read the following passages to further reflect upon the truths from this session.*

Deuteronomy 6

Joshua 1

Psalm 119-1-56

Psalm 119:57-104

Psalm 119:105-176

**What insight do these passages reveal about the Word of God?**

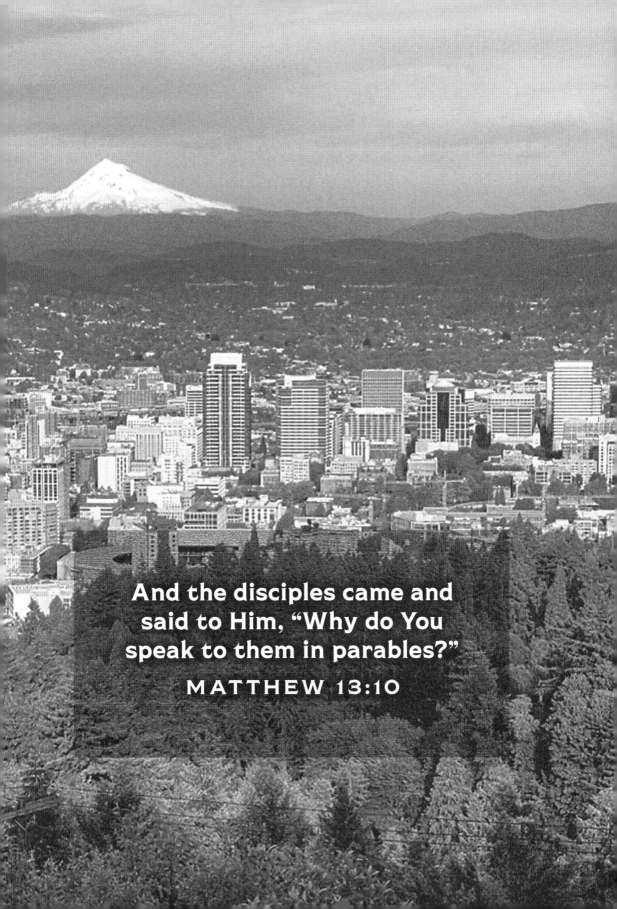

And the disciples came and said to Him, "Why do You speak to them in parables?"

MATTHEW 13:10

# THE GOD WHO SPEAKS

In this session, Pastor Daniel discussed how all people want to hear God speak to them. The good news is, we serve a God who communicates with His people. From the opening chapters of Genesis through the Book of Revelation, we see evidence that God is committed to speaking to those who want to hear. As modern-day believers, the primary way we hear from God is through His Word. The Bible itself has a lot to say about the role the Scriptures should play in the life of a believer.

*Read 2 Timothy 3:16-17.*

**List everything these verses say about the Scriptures.**

**What does it mean when Paul writes Scripture is inspired by God?**

**According to these verses, what is Scripture able to do?**

In Paul's letter to Timothy, he revealed that the Scriptures were "inspired" by God—which means "breathed out by God." When Paul referred to the Scriptures he was referring to the Old Testament, but by implication, he was referring to the New Testament as well. When the Bible was written, God spoke through more than 40 authors over a period of 1500 years. As you read the Scriptures, you'll notice the individual styles and personalities of the authors are apparent in the text, but God inspired the words Himself. Because Scripture originated with God, it's profitable for us to interact with it regularly. It is necessary for us to know God and know how we are supposed to live.

# Living and Powerful

*Read Hebrews 4:12.*

How does the author of Hebrews describe the Word of God?

What does it mean when the author reveals that God's Word "pierces even to the division of soul and spirit, and of joints and marrow?"

In the same way a surgeon's knife pierces into the deepest parts of a person's body, the Word of God probes into our innermost thoughts, attitudes, and emotions. God's Word delivers both bad and good news. The bad news is that because of our sin, all human beings have fallen short of the glory of God (Rom. 3:23). The good news is that because of His grace, God has provided a way for us to be reconciled to Him through the finished work of Jesus Christ on the cross. In other words, God's Word serves to convict us of our sins and also offers us a pardon, resurrection, and life for those who believe in Jesus.

When is the first time you realized you had a sin problem that separated you from God? What brought you to that conclusion?

What role do the Scriptures play in your relationship with God?

Bible reading is one of the most important habits we can engage in because it puts us in a posture to grow in our faith. As we continue in this study of the parables, spend time thinking about the truths you are learning and how to apply them to your life.

# Personal Study 2
# UNDERSTANDING PARABLES

The Bible is filled with writings from many different genres. The Bible contains narratives, prophecy, poetry, Major and Minor Prophets, wisdom literature, the Gospels, and Epistles. Within the Gospels, Jesus used a method of storytelling we know as the parables. In the parables, Jesus often used a familiar subject to teach an unfamiliar spiritual truth.

*Read Matthew 13:10-17,34-35.*

**Glance back at verse 10. What did the disciples ask Jesus?**


Jesus' words were visually stimulating. For example, He spoke of a camel attempting to go through the eye of a needle (Matt. 19:24). He warned against a "divided house" (Mark 3:25), the "yeast" of the Pharisees (Mark 8:15), and people attempting to remove "specks" from other's eyes when there were planks in their own (Matt. 7:5). Undoubtedly, Jesus' disciples were aware of His vibrant communication style. But after He told them the parable of the sower (a parable we will study next week), His disciples asked Him: "Why do You speak to them in parables?" (13:10).

**How did Jesus answer their question?**


**Does Jesus' response seem shocking to you? Why or why not?**


Jesus spoke in parables so that those who God wants to know His truth, will know. Now, doesn't that sound kind of strange? I mean, think about that for a second. Jesus spoke these stories, these thrown alongside tales so that the people who God wants to understand will understand and subsequently the people who don't want to understand won't. Now doesn't that surprise you? It surprises me. I remember the first time I read this, I thought to myself, "Wait a second. So God doesn't want everyone to know?" Initially, Jesus' response might seem harsh, but in reality it was an act of mercy. A greater exposure to the truth increases one's accountability toward God in judgment (Matt. 11:20-24), so concealing the truth may have been an act of grace to those who He knew would be unresponsive. But take another look at Jesus' words about those who believe:

> *But blessed are your eyes for they see, and your ears for*
> *they hear; for assuredly, I say to you that many prophets*
> *and righteous men desired to see what you see, and did not*
> *see it, and to hear what you hear, and did not hear it.*
> MATTHEW 13:16-17

When people hear and believe the Word of God and trust in God's grace to save them, God imparts more and more truth to them in which they can live by. All believers have the ability to understand even the deep things of God because the Holy Spirit is faithful to impart truth to those who belong to Him (1 Cor. 2:9-10).

**At this point, how would you describe your level of confidence in learning new things in Scripture?**

Jesus' disciples were ordinary men. They were not scribes, experts in Old Testament law, Rabbis, or theologians. They were common people with ordinary jobs and yet they understood the spiritual truths Jesus taught them. In the same way, modern-day believers don't need special skills or advanced degrees to understand the truths of God's Word. The Bible is for everyone, and if you will commit to studying, the Holy Spirit will be faithful to teach you.

**Close your time today praying that God would work through the Spirit to enable you to understand the truths of His Word.**

# Personal Study 3
# FULFILLING PROPHECY

In the previous personal study session, we unpacked a couple of the reasons Jesus taught in parables. We learned that Jesus spoke in parables so those were willing would hear and believe. Secondly, He spoke in parables to conceal truth from those who He knew would reject it. In today's study, we'll look at another reason why Jesus taught in parables.

**Read the passage below.**

*All these things Jesus spoke to the multitude in parables; and*
*without a parable He did not speak to them, that it might*
*be fulfilled which was spoken by the prophet, saying:*
*"I will open My mouth in parables;*
*I will utter things kept secret from the foundation of the world."*
MATTHEW 13:34-35

**According to this passage, what's the third reason Jesus spoke in parables?**

**Look up Psalm 78:2. How does this passage relate to Matthew 13:34-35?**

Everything about Jesus' life and ministry was in alignment with Scripture. Jesus is the fulfillment of Scripture—even down to the words that came out of His mouth, and the way He communicated spiritual truth to those who were willing to hear. Jesus is still communicating through His Word today. If you want to understand Scripture, ask God to increase your understanding. If you're one of His followers, He delights to increase your understanding because you're one of those people He wants to know and He wants to reveal Himself to you.

**Read the passage below.**

*And He said, "Go, and tell this people:*
*'Keep on hearing, but do not understand;*
*Keep on seeing, but do not perceive.'*
*"Make the heart of this people dull,*
*And their ears heavy,*
*And shut their eyes;*
*Lest they see with their eyes,*
*And hear with their ears,*
*And understand with their heart,*
*And return and be healed."*
ISAIAH 6:9-10

**What is the relationship between understanding God's Word and being willing to obey God's Word?**

**Why might it be tempting merely to take God's Word in as information, but not a Word from God that can and should change our lives?**

**How should we respond when we're tempted to not obey God's Word?**

The people the prophet Isaiah described in the verses above were not impacted by the Word of God. They had an obedience problem. You and I have to make sure we're not in that place, because don't miss the fact Jesus was talking about some very religious people who took their religion practice very seriously. Ultimately this was the same group of people who would crucify Him. They knew about Jesus but they didn't know Him as their Lord. Have you ever seen a Christian who's acting nothing like a Christian but thinks that they are? We want to avoid that at all costs. But asking God for revelation is asking God to orient all of your human faculties to be able to understand and perceive who God is and what He's done and what He's doing.

# The Parable of the Soils

# GROUP STUDY

## Start

*Welcome everyone to session 2.*

In popular culture, the "heart" has been the topic of countless love songs, books, and movies. We've all heard the cliché, "Follow your heart." We consider the heart to be the driving force of our passions and emotions. So it's interesting to learn what the Bible has to say about our heart. King Solomon wrote:

> *Keep your heart with all diligence,*
> *For out of it spring the issues of life.*
> PROVERBS 4:23

So "Keep your heart" while other translations say, "Guard your heart." Why do you think the author of Proverbs instructed us to "keep/guard our hearts?"

You've probably heard someone say, "His heart isn't in the right place." What do they mean when they say that?

Practically speaking, how can we "guard our heart" as the author of Proverbs instructed?

*Pray and ask God to use your time together.*
*After praying, watch the video teaching.*

# 𝔚𝔞𝔱𝔠𝔥

*Use the space below to take notes
while you watch video session 2.*

To access the teaching sessions,
use the instructions in the back
of your Bible study book.

# Discuss

The parable of the soils is a story Jesus told about four different types of "soils" or conditions of the heart—a hard heart, shallow heart, worldly heart, or a heart that is open to God. On any given day our hearts might be in any (or all) of these states. Jesus told this story to help us identify ways our hearts may be closed off to His work in our hearts and in the world.

*Read Matthew 13:1-9,18-23 together.*

1.  Of the four states of the heart described in this session, which do you struggle with most often? What does that look like?

2.  God has given us a parable like this to help us keep our own heart with diligence. What are some identifiers that your heart is getting hard, shallow or worldly?

3.  What are some common triggers that draw your heart into hard, shallow, and worldly places? How do you address these stressors when they appear? How might you proactively address these known stressors?

4.  How can the desire to be liked or be successful keep us from being fruitful in the way that God intends?

5.  What are practical ways to tend to your heart and redirect it back to the right place?

6.  How do you know when your heart is spiritually in a good place? Is your attitude or behavior different? If so, how?

*Close your discussion with prayer. Remind those in your group to complete the personal studies and Bible reading over the next week.*

# Reading Plan

*Over the next week, read the following passages to further reflect upon the truths from this session.*

Jeremiah 17:1-13

Ezekiel 36:22-37

Matthew 12:33-37

Jeremiah 31:31-34

Ephesians 3:1-20

**What do these Scriptures teach you about the heart?**

Then He spoke many things
to them in parables, saying:
"Behold, a sower went out to sow."

MATTHEW 13:3

# Personal Study 1
# HOW'S YOUR HEART?

In last week's study, we discussed how Jesus used parables when He taught and we unpacked some of the reasons He did so. This week, we'll look at our first parable which is known as the parable of the soils.

*Read Matthew 13:1-9.*

**Who was Jesus speaking to when He taught this parable? (v. 2) Why is that important?**

**How did the soils where the seeds are planted affect the fruitfulness of the seed?**

Jesus often used familiar concepts to explain unfamiliar spiritual truths. In the first century, Jesus ministered in an agrarian culture, so it's not surprising He used a farming example to illustrate a spiritual principle. In the parable of the soils, Jesus identified four potential types of soil that represent the human heart and He explained the parable in further detail.

## A Hard Heart
*Read Matthew 13:18-23.*

The four types of soils that Jesus mentions represent potential conditions of the human heart: a hard heart (v. 19), shallow heart (v. 20-21), worldly heart (v. 22), or open heart that's receptive to God's truth (v. 23). So here's the thing: One quality of the soil of your heart that you're keeping is that you could have a hard heart. And because you have a hard heart, God's Word can't get in. You don't understand it. It sits on the surface. And you know what they call seed that's on the surface—bird food.

**What outside influences contribute to having a hard heart?**

**How do we learn to recognize when our hearts are becoming hard?**

All of us have the capacity to have hardness in our hearts. A lot of times, that hardness is formed by people stepping on it. If you've had enough bad stuff go on, it's natural for your heart to get hard. For some of us, the circumstances of our lives have made us hard. Maybe it was a bad relationships or situation. Maybe people did awful things to you. The problem with hard-heartedness is that there's no room for the seed (which represents God's truth) to get in at all. The seed sits on the surface and is exactly what the enemy Satan wants, because the Word of God can't get in and change you. It sits on the surface and gets nowhere.

**What steps can you take to deal with any hardness you might have in your heart?**

**What role does prayer play in dealing with a hard heart?**

The problem with hardness of heart is that it's not fruitful. Prayer will be a key factor in avoiding a hard heart. So you have to say, "Lord, will You do a work on me? Lord, will You break up the hard areas of my life?" In our prayer life, we have to continually pray for spiritual growth and maturing. As we continue our study of the parables, we'd do well to pray for our hearts to be open to God's Word and fruitful for the kingdom of God.

# HOW'S YOUR HEART?
## PART 2

In the previous personal study, we introduced the various types of soils that Jesus spoke of in the parable of the soils. In today's study, we'll continue to look at more potential conditions of the heart.

# A shallow heart

*Read the passage below.*

*But he who received the seed on stony places, this is he who hears the word and immediately receives it with joy; yet he has no root in himself, but endures only for a while. For when tribulation or persecution arises because of the word, immediately he stumbles.*
MATTHEW 13:20-21

We live in a shallow culture that focuses more on outer appearances rather than inner depth. Sadly, the same thing can happen in our faith. What do I mean by shallowness? There's no roots there. You start to grow in your faith, but the troubles of life usher in a storm and because your faith lacks deep roots, the storms of life drench the soil of our hearts and washout and uproot the seeds that were planted. Our spiritual lives need depth to thrive.

**What areas of your faith need greater depth?**

**Where are you at risk for being shallow?**

We don't want to be shallow. You know what one of my goals is? To keep standing up for Jesus because I watch people come and go all the time. They get real fired up but then fizzle out and fall away. I just want to keep showing up. I don't want to be the person where the fruit's born and then right as things get hard, the fruits go and wither away. I want to be deep in the things of God. I don't want it to just be on the surface. Every day is a day for God to deepen us, to take us into the next place if we're willing, but your heart has to be willing. You have to be willing to say, "Lord, bring me out of the shallow ground today. I don't want my faith to be shallow."

# A Worldly Heart

*Read the passage below.*

*Now he who received seed among the thorns is he who hears the word, and the cares of this world and the deceitfulness of riches choke the word, and he becomes unfruitful.*
MATTHEW 13:22

**According to the passage above, what are two things that choke out the Word of God and cause a person to be unfruitful?**

**What are the main distractions that put you at risk for a worldly heart?**

**What steps can you take to prevent a worldly heart?**

No one sets out to have a worldly heart, but if we aren't careful the fast pace and the stress of life can distract us to the point it impacts our faith. Notice how Jesus mentioned the "cares of the world" and the "deceitfulness of riches." We can get so caught up in day-to-do living and the pursuit of making a living that we forget what matters most. Of course, we have to be responsible—to tend to our responsibilities and to earn money live, but we must be careful not to disregard our faith in the process.

# AN OPEN HEART: RECEPTIVE TO GOD'S WORD

We've already discussed what it means to have a hard, shallow, and worldly heart. In today's personal study, we'll learn what it means to have a heart that is receptive to God's Word—the kind that bears fruit.

## 100 Fold Harvest

*Read the passage below.*

*But he who received seed on the good ground is he who hears the word and understands it, who indeed bears fruit and produces: some a hundredfold, some sixty, some thirty.*
MATTHEW 13:23

**What are signs of an open heart that is receptive to God's Word?**

**In your experience, how is life different when your heart is in a place where it is open and receptive to God's Word?**

**According to verse 23, how much fruit is possible in the life of a believer? Why should we take note of the different amounts?**

Jesus wants us to be fruitful. He wants His good Word that He sows in our hearts to land on good ground unencumbered, not by hardness, not by rocks that make it shallow, and not by other species that choke out the fruit. He says, "I want you to be fruitful." But you might be thinking, "How do I get an open heart that bears fruit?" That's an excellent question and one Jesus has answered for us.

# Abiding Produces Fruit

*Read the passage below.*

*I am the vine, you are the branches. He who abides in Me, and I in him, bears much fruit; for without Me you can do nothing. If anyone does not abide in Me, he is cast out as a branch and is withered; and they gather them and throw them into the fire, and they are burned. If you abide in Me, and My words abide in you, you will ask what you desire, and it shall be done for you. By this My Father is glorified, that you bear much fruit; so you will be My disciples.*
JOHN 15:5-8

**What does it mean to abide in something? What does it mean to abide in Jesus?**

**Glance back at verse 5. Why is it essential that we are always connected to Jesus? What happens when we disconnect from Him?**

**According to this passage, with the Christian life comes an expectation of fruit. How does that make you feel?**

For each one of us, the goal is to abide in Jesus. The goal is to have a heart receptive to God's Word and a life that produces fruit in a way that brings glory to the kingdom of God. A hard, shallow, or worldly heart is a threat to our progress, so we have to be mindful of the state of our heart. Abiding in Jesus through Bible reading, prayer, and worship is the key to having a receptive heart that produces fruit.

# SESSION 3
# The Parable of Lost Things

# GROUP STUDY

## Start

*Welcome everyone to session 3.*

Have you ever lost something that caused you to panic? What was it? How did you respond when you realized it was missing?

What items are you most careful to keep track of? What makes these things important?

*Read the passage below.*

*For the Son of Man has come to seek and to save that which was lost.*
LUKE 19:10

How does this passage help us understand what Jesus values?

God cares deeply for the lost. So much so, that Jesus' entire reason for coming was to seek the lost and reconcile them to the Father. In this week's lesson, we'll take a look at the parable of the lost coin and the lost sheep found in Luke 15.

*Pray and ask God to use your time together.*
*After praying, watch the video teaching.*

# 𝔚atch

*Use the space below to take notes
while you watch video session 3.*

To access the teaching sessions,
use the instructions in the back
of your Bible study book.

# Discuss

*Use the following questions to guide
your discussion of the video.*

God loves lost things. We know this because when God loses something He values, He chooses to go look for it. To illustrate this point, Jesus told two stories about two lost objects—the parables of the lost coin and the lost sheep. These stories Jesus told give us valuable insight into what God treasures.

*Read Luke 15:1-10 together.*

1.  Respond to this statement: Something doesn't lose it's value when it's lost; it retains value even when it's missing. How have you found this to be true? How is this especially true for people made in God's image?

2.  How does the previous statement challenge the way we tend to think about people who are far from God?

3.  Though every person is made in God's image, every person has been warped by sin. How can these things be true at the same time?

4.  What changes in our hearts when we begin to see every person is of infinite value to God?

5.  How do we cultivate hearts that love people as much as God does? Practically speaking, what does it look like to love people like God does?

6.  In both parables, when the lost item is found, the person rejoices. How should worship fuel our desire to help lost people find Jesus?

*Close your discussion with prayer. Remind those in your group to complete the personal studies and Bible reading over the next week.*

# Reading Plan

*Over the next week, read the following passages to further reflect upon the truths from this session.*

Romans 10

Isaiah 61

Luke 19:1-10

Isaiah 52

Matthew 28:16-20

**What do these passages teach about sharing the gospel?**

What man of you, having a hundred sheep, if he loses one of them, does not leave the ninety-nine in the wilderness, and go after the one which is lost until he finds it?

LUKE 15:4

## Personal Study 1

# THE PARABLE OF THE LOST SHEEP

If you've ever lost or misplaced something important, you know how alarming it is when you realize it's missing and what lengths you'll go to attempt to get it back. In today's passage, Jesus tells the parable of the lost sheep, and in this story, we get a good look at the heart of God.

*Read Luke 15:1-7.*

**According to verses 1-2, who was Jesus telling the parable to?**

**What does it tell us about the shepherd to know that he was willing to leave 99 sheep to search for the one?**

**When have you been concerned about the value of a lost object?**

# A Diverse Crowd

Jesus was speaking to a diverse crowd of people. The text tells us there were "tax collectors and sinners" as well as "Pharisees and scribes" who had gathered to hear Jesus speak (Luke 15:1-2). In Jesus' day, tax collectors and sinners were the two most maligned groups of people amongst the religious people. These were people who lived in such a way that was offensive to the religious elite. And yet, Jesus had also drawn the attention of the Pharisees and scribes— and He taught both groups the same message.

**What do the diverse crowd and Jesus' message to them reveal about the heart of God?**

**Glance back at verse 2. What did the Pharisees say about Jesus? How should this reality impact who we welcome to our tables and spheres of influence?**

This story reveals God's love for the lost. Why does He love the lost? Because He created them. Every single human being, no matter where they are in their spiritual journey, they've been created by God and they are His image-bearers. And all of us, at some point, were lost and disconnected from God. Notice how Jesus told the story to both the outcasts and the religious elite. No person or group was excluded from Jesus' circle.

*Read the passage below.*

*For God so loved the world that He gave His only begotten Son, that whoever believes in Him should not perish but have everlasting life. For God did not send His Son into the world to condemn the world, but that the world through Him might be saved.*
JOHN 3:16-17

**How does this passage impact the way you view those who are not-yet believers in Jesus?**

Jesus' mission was to save the world. But keep in mind that loving the lost and being with them doesn't mean He partook of all the things they partook of. He was willing to be present, but He never participated in sin. Being around lost people will not taint us—it did not taint Jesus. Here's what I want to tell you— Jesus loves you just as you are, but He loves you too much to leave you like that. We all show up and Jesus receives us, and then Jesus starts to get to work on us. Jesus says, "I want to do a work in your life; I want to transform your life." Our role is simply to keep responding to Jesus.

# THE PARABLE OF THE LOST COIN

In yesterday's study, we discussed God's love for the lost by looking at the parable of the lost sheep. Today we'll continue our study with the parable of the lost coin.

*Read the passage below.*

*Or what woman, having ten silver coins, if she loses one coin, does not light a lamp, sweep the house, and search carefully until she finds it? And when she has found it, she calls her friends and neighbors together, saying, 'Rejoice with me, for I have found the piece which I lost!' Likewise, I say to you, there is joy in the presence of the angels of God over one sinner who repents.*
LUKE 15:8-10

**How intentionally did the woman seek the coin? What does this communicate about its value?**

**What did the woman do when she found the coin? Why do you think she called her friends?**

**How does Jesus parallel the woman's joy to heaven's response when one sinner repents?**

# Valuable To God

This coin, known as a drachma, was worth about one day's wages, so the woman wanted to look for it—she wasn't content to say, "Well, at least I still have nine coins." Understandably, she wanted all ten in her possession. The greater spiritual point at work in this parable is that the object maintained its value to the owner, even though it was lost. The owner was willing to drop everything and search for the lost item. In the same way, lost people are valuable because they maintain the image of God. God loves us, is willing to pursue us, and to bring us back into His possession. God was so committed to our redemption He sent His only Son to die on a cross to make reconciliation possible (John 3:16-17).

**Have you ever experienced a time when you felt worthless? How does this parable challenge that notion?**

**According to this story, what gives us our value? Why should we not base our value on achievement, success, or any other cultural marker?**

**How would you describe what it means to repent?**

The lost get found when they realize they're separated from God and in need of repentance. Now, repentance is what happens when you simply respond to Jesus. Another way of saying it is, repentance is a change of mind that leads to a change of heart, which leads to a change of direction. See, when that happens, it says that all of heaven rejoices (Luke 15:10). There will be more joy in heaven, over one sinner who repents than over 99 just persons who need no repentance. Jesus loves the lost so much He came to earth to seek and find them. When He finds the lost all of heaven rejoices. The Christian life is about seeking the lost.

## Personal Study 3

# GOD'S HEART
# FOR THE LOST

In the previous two personal studies, we looked at the parable of the lost sheep and the parable of the lost coin. We learned that God loves the lost and lost people have great value to God. In today's study, we'll answer the question: what does that mean for us?

*Read the passage below.*

*"Go therefore and make disciples of all the nations, baptizing them in the name of the Father and of the Son and of the Holy Spirit, teaching them to observe all things that I have commanded you; and lo, I am with you always, even to the end of the age." Amen.*
MATTHEW 28:19-20

**What comes to mind when you think about sharing your faith with people who don't know God?**

**What obstacles keep you from telling people about Jesus?**

# Love God, Love People

We tend to overcomplicate sharing our faith, but it's simpler than you think. If you will invest and engage with the people around you, build relationships, be a good neighbor, be friendly at your job, talk about Jesus, share your story, and invite people to church—I promise you that your everyday lifestyle will proclaim the good news of Jesus, and you will persuade people to believe it.

Yet one of the reasons we don't share our faith is because we get comfortable being part of the 99 sheep who aren't lost. We feel safe and have plenty of relationships, and you've found your place in biblical community, and that's a beautiful thing. But I believe God wants all of us to be reproducing spiritually. We need to be open and be out in the community. Do you know what happens when you get out in the community? God uses you in powerful ways.

**Do you feel connected to a local church family? If so, what steps can you take to get active in biblical community?**

**If you're "one of the 99"—meaning someone settled in the Christian community, in what areas of your life have you become stagnant in getting out of your sphere of influence and building new relationships for the sake of the gospel?**

When you stay open to new experiences and make it a point to continue to build relationships, you become a catalyst for growth for all sorts of people. Before you know it, people are like, listen, "I don't believe what you believe, but can you pray for me?" When that happens, you know you're a light in a dark world. God loves the lost, and as His followers, we are to love the lost. We're not here to condemn the world. The world is condemned already. Jesus came to save the lost, so we're not here to drag down the world—it's already pulled down. We are here to love God and love people.

**Who do you know who is "the one" as opposed to "the 99"?**

**What might it look like to seek them out and be present with them the way God was and is with you?**

# The Parable of the Wheat and Weeds

# GROUP STUDY

## Start

*Welcome everyone to session 4.*

We all have expectations. We may or may not communicate them well, but we have expectations with family members, friends, coworkers, and even people at church. When our expectations aren't met, we usually feel disappointed and maybe even angry.

**What are common expectations shared by most people?**

**How do you respond when your expectations aren't met?**

**Have you ever set unreasonable expectations? If so, how did you learn they were unreasonable?**

In addition to the exceptions we place on our family and friends, we also have expectations—whether we acknowledge them or not—about church. The parable of the wheat and the weeds gives us helpful information for managing our expectations and living within a church that can often be messy.

*Pray and ask God to use your time together.*
*After praying, watch the video teaching.*

# 𝔚𝔞𝔱𝔠𝔥

*Use the space below to take notes
while you watch video session 4.*

To access the teaching sessions,
use the instructions in the back
of your Bible study book.

# Discuss

*Use the following questions to guide
your discussion of the video.*

Expectations ruin relationships because if expectations aren't known and shared they put pressure on every relationship and situation we encounter—this is also true of the church. This is why the story Jesus told about the wheat and the weeds is important for us to hear and digest. He mentioned some of the reasons we get disappointed at church; we are all sinners in need of grace, sometimes people act poorly, and sometimes we have unrealistic expectations.

*Read Matthew 13:24-30 together.*

1.  How should it make us feel to realize that not everyone in the life of a church belongs to God? Why is knowing this important?

2.  On the other hand, why should we focus on bearing fruit rather than finding and pulling up weeds?

3.  What types of things cause disappointment in church life? How can this parable help us manage our expectations at church as well as our other relationships with other Christians?

4.  Read John 10:10. How have you seen this strategy from Satan play out?

5.  Most of the people in a church are people in the process of growth. How can we nurture these people to become healthy and fruitful?

6.  Why might it be helpful to give people permission to speak truths into our lives while we're in process together?

*Close your discussion with prayer. Remind those in your group to
complete the personal studies and Bible reading over the next week.*

# Reading Plan

*Over the next week, read the following passages to further reflect upon the truths from this session.*

Genesis 3

John 3

Matthew 10:16-25

Matthew 25:31-46

1 John 4

**What do these Scriptures reveal about the presence of good and evil in the world?**

Another parable He put forth to them, saying: "The kingdom of heaven is like a man who sowed good seed in his field; but while men slept, his enemy came and sowed tares among the wheat and went his way."

MATTHEW 13:24-25

# Personal Study 1
# THE PARABLE OF THE WHEAT AND WEEDS

This week, we'll continue study with Jesus' parable of the wheat and weeds. Again, we see Jesus using a teaching illustration that pertains to agriculture—a topic His audience would've fully understood. In this parable, Jesus warns of Satan's strategies to hinder the work of God.

Read the passage below.

> Another parable He put forth to them, saying: "The kingdom of heaven is like a man who sowed good seed in his field; but while men slept, his enemy came and sowed tares among the wheat and went his way. But when the grain had sprouted and produced a crop, then the tares also appeared. So the servants of the owner came and said to him, 'Sir, did you not sow good seed in your field? How then does it have tares?' He said to them, 'An enemy has done this.' The servants said to him, 'Do you want us then to go and gather them up?' But he said, 'No, lest while you gather up the tares you also uproot the wheat with them. Let both grow together until the harvest, and at the time of harvest I will say to the reapers, 'First gather together the tares and bind them in bundles to burn them, but gather the wheat into my barn.'"
> MATTHEW 13:24-30

**What does the farmer's field in this parable represent? Who does the man's enemy represent?**

**Why couldn't the farmer differentiate between the wheat and the weeds?**

Why was the farmer careful to not pull of the weeds immediately?

# 𝔚𝔥𝔢𝔞𝔱 & 𝔚𝔢𝔢𝔡𝔰: 𝔅𝔢𝔩𝔦𝔢𝔳𝔢𝔯𝔰 & 𝔘𝔫𝔟𝔢𝔩𝔦𝔢𝔳𝔢𝔯𝔰

In this parable, Jesus compares the kingdom of heaven to a farmer who sowed good seed in his field, but then an enemy came in behind him and sowed weeds. The weeds Jesus spoke of could have been a plant called darnel. Today, most people are unfamiliar with darnel, but in Jesus' day, His audience would've been familiar. Darnel is a plant that is related to wheat and looks similar, but unlike wheat, darnel is poisonous. Roman law forbid sowing darnel in someone else's field. Wheat and darnel become intertwined at the root, and it's difficult to uproot the weeds without damaging the wheat. So to protect the wheat, a wise farmer allows the two to grow together.

**Have you ever experienced a situation when there were "good and bad things" mixed together? If so, what was it?**

**Identify a few key truths this parable illustrates about the life of the church.**

**How does this parable help us adjust our expectations for the church?**

# THE PARABLE OF THE WHEAT & WEEDS PART 2

In our previous personal study, the parable of the wheat and weeds was introduced. Jesus told a story about a man who planted wheat in a field and an enemy came in behind him and planted weeds. In today's study, we'll unpack what spiritual truths Jesus intended to convey in the story.

*Read Matthew 13:36-42.*

**Glance back at verse 36. Why did the disciples approach Jesus?**

**How do you respond when you encounter something in the Bible you don't understand?**

**Why do we often neglect to go to Jesus like the disciples did when we don't understand Scripture?**

The disciples went to Jesus with their questions about the parable. We believe in Jesus, but too many of us don't go to the Word of God or to prayer with our questions. Some of you think about the questions in your own minds and we go to our friends, or some of you, your idea of getting advice is going on social media and then you're at the mercy of your peer group. Now, you have to realize that in the Bible, being at the mercy of the wisdom of your peer group always ends up in calamity. Of course, if you have a wise and godly mentor, it's a good idea to discuss the Scriptures and asks questions with that person. But the point is, we'd do well to follow the lead of the disciples and converse with Jesus in prayer and seek His Word for the answers to the questions we are asking.

# Good and Evil

When Jesus' disciples approached Him asking questions about the parable He'd told, He explained that the wheat and weeds represent good and evil in the world. Many Jews who'd been waiting for the coming of the Messiah anticipated that when He came, He would immediately eradicate evil from the world—but that wasn't God's plan. So, some were confused and questioned Jesus' authority. But in this parable, Jesus demonstrated He was not the source of evil. The entire world belongs to God and the enemy has no right to bring evil into the world, and the Son of God will assert His authority over the world at the time of judgment. But for now, there's a combination of both good and evil in the world.

> How does knowing there is both good and evil in the world help us manage our expectations?

> Why should we not be surprised when bad or alarming things happen, even in church?

> Glance back at Matthew 13:41-42. According to these verses, how will evil be dealt with at the time of judgment?

A time is coming on the kingdom calendar when God will judge all sin. Then, every sin ever committed will either be covered by the blood of Christ, or the person who committed the sin will stand in judgment before God—there will be no exceptions. Until then, it is our responsibility to abide in Jesus and be on guard against evil.

# OPPOSITION IS TO BE EXPECTED

In this week's study of the parable of the wheat and weeds we've discussed the fact that we live in a world filled with both good and evil. Satan is opposed to God's rule on earth and he does everything in his power to oppose it. Satan even goes as far as to mix counterfeit Christians among true Christians to hinder God's work. Our role as Christians is to be alert and aware.

*Read the passage below.*

*And no wonder! For Satan himself transforms himself into an angel of light. Therefore it is no great thing if his ministers also transform themselves into ministers of righteousness, whose end will be according to their works.*
2 CORINTHIANS 11:14-15

**According to the apostle Paul, what does Satan transform himself into? (v. 14). Why is this particularly deceiving to believers?**

**If Satan has the ability to deceive by appearing good, in what other areas of life are deception possible?**

According to the apostle Paul, Satan and his agents have the ability to deceive believers by appearing to be something they aren't—good and full of light. That doesn't mean everyone we disagree with at church is an unbeliever. Keep in mind, even true Christians still sin and act poorly sometimes. But we must remember that not everyone associated with the church loves God.

*Read the passage below.*

*The thief does not come except to steal, and to
kill, and to destroy. I have come that they may have
life, and that they may have it more abundantly.*
JOHN 10:10

**How did Jesus describe Satan's mission in this passage?**

**How does Jesus' plan for us differ from the enemy's?**

**How does it impact you when you contemplate that Satan has a plan
for your life that is very different from God's plan?**

# Abundant Life

Satan has come to steal, kill, and destroy us, but Jesus' plan for us is to live an
abundant life. The church isn't perfect and we can't always distinguish believers
from non-believers but that doesn't mean we should avoid church life. A day
is coming when distinctions will be made. Until then, it is our role to abide in
Christ and stay in Christian fellowship. We should never be ignorant of the
enemy's plan to wreak havoc. But if we were to drop out of church life we'd be
allowing the enemy to steal the community of true believers God intends for us
to have and enjoy. Instead, we are to be active in a community of believers and
to stay alert and wise to the enemy's schemes.

# SESSION 5

# The Parable of the Prodigal Son

# GROUP STUDY

## 𝔖tart

*Welcome everyone to session 5.*

Each year countless self-help books are written that teach readers how to avoid wasting time, money, energy, and other precious resources because we all squander resources in one way or another. When a commodity is considered valuable, a wise person learns to manage that commodity with care and to get the most out of it.

**What comes to mind when you think about wasted resources?**

**In what area of life are you most inclined to waste or squander something valuable?**

**How would you describe what it means to be a good steward of something?**

While we all understand ways we waste time, money, and energy, fewer of us consider the ways we waste spiritual resources. In this week's study, we'll look at the parable of the prodigal son and consider how we might be squandering our relationship with the Father.

*Pray and ask God to use your time together.*
*After praying, watch the video teaching.*

# Watch

*Use the space below to take notes
while you watch video session 5.*

To access the teaching sessions,
use the instructions in the back
of your Bible study book.

# Discuss

*Use the following questions to guide
your discussion of the video.*

One of the most amazing things about Jesus is how deeply His teaching has permeated our culture. Most people, regardless of their faith, are familiar with what Christians call the Great Commandment. The same can said for many of the stories Jesus told. This session, we will look more deeply at one of Jesus' best known teachings—the parable of the prodigal son.

*Read Luke 15:11-32 together.*

1.  There are actually two sons in the parable who squander the love of their father. It's obvious how the younger son (the prodigal) squandered his father's love and resources. But how is the older brother guilty of the same?

2.  Which brother in the parable do you most identify with? Why?

3.  Why do you think it is more socially acceptable to be like the older brother? Why might there be even greater spiritual danger for the older brother?

4.  How can you have an active church life with the appearance of spiritual health and still miss the heart of God?

5.  No mistake we can make is greater than the grace of God. What is this story meant to teach about the grace and love of God the Father? When have you experienced the kind of lavish love from God described in this parable?

6.  Every sinner has a past and every saint has a future. How can we use our stories to be lights and signposts for other prodigals?

*Close your discussion with prayer. Remind those in your group to
complete the personal studies and Bible reading over the next week.*

Video sessions available at lifeway.com/stories

# 𝕽eading 𝕻lan

*Over the next week, read the following passages to further reflect upon the truths from this session.*

Matthew 3

Luke 5:27-31

Acts 26:12-20

Romans 2:1-16

2 Corinthians 7

**What do these passages reveal about repentance?**

Then He said: "A certain man had two sons. And the younger of them said to his father, 'Father, give me the portion of goods that falls to me.' So he divided to them his livelihood."

LUKE 15:11-12

# THE PRODIGAL SON

## When Desperation is a Gift

The story of the prodigal son is perhaps Jesus' most well-known parable. It will be familiar to some of you and perhaps others will be studying it for the first time. Either way, ask God to shed new light on this parable and for a greater understanding of the heart of God.

*Read Luke 15:11-24.*

**Why might the younger son's request for his inheritance be insulting to the Father?**

**Glance back at verses 13-16. What series of events led to the prodigal's dire situation?**

**Spiritually speaking, why was the young man's desperation actually a blessing?**

The younger son had done a terrible thing by asking for an early inheritance from his father. It was the equivalent of saying, "I want the things you can give me, but I don't want you." An inheritance is normally bestowed upon the grantor's death. And still, the father granted the foolish young man's request. Soon, the prodigal was out of money. To complicate matters, a famine struck the land. Sin never satisfies the way we think it will and the inconveniences of life seldom let up. Before long, the prodigal had sunk so low he wished he were eating pig pods and wished for the status of one of his father's hired servants.

The future looked bleak for the prodigal but from a spiritual standpoint, things were looking up. Oftentimes, desperation causes us to come to our senses.

**What dire circumstances or chain of events have motivated you to seek God?**

**Why do we often neglect God until we find circumstances we can't overcome on our own?**

This young man's story shows what happens when we stray from God and squander what He's given us. Unfortunately, some of us know what this is like. Some of us know what it's like to be so far away from God and so given over to things that are so wasteful and excessive, that before you know it, pigs' food looks delicious.

**In what ways do you identify with the prodigal?**

**Why do you think hardship has a way of bringing us to our senses?**

But then all of a sudden, notice what the text says in verse 17. "And he arose and he came to his father." In the depths of his misery, the young man came to his senses and made a plan to return home to his father. It's the first wise choice we've seen him make and it's exactly what he needed to get himself headed in the right direction.

**What must this young man have known about his father to return to him?**

# THE LOVE OF THE FATHER

In the previous personal study, we took a look at the story of the prodigal son. We watched the prodigal leave home, squander his father's resources, and then he found himself in need. At the end of our study, the prodigal had come to his senses and wanted to return to his father as a hired hand. In today's study, we'll see how the father responds to his return.

*Read Luke 15:25-31.*

**Glance back at verse 20. What does this suggest the father was doing as the son was headed home? What do the father's actions tell us about the father?**

**Why was the son unable to finish the speech he had rehearsed for his father?**

## Embraced and Celebrated

Here's the thing. Your return is embraced and celebrated. Keep in mind that Jesus is talking to the Pharisees about the people who were considered the riff-raff of the day. He's saying, "Listen, you get lost when you leave and squander. But when you come back, you are embraced and celebrated." Jesus is saying, "You guys don't realize you've missed the very heart of God." Why? "Because these tax collectors, they're coming back and I am embracing them and I'm celebrating the fact that they are interested in the kingdom of God again." The father had been waiting and watching for his son to come home—that's why he spotted him while he was still a long way off. And the father ran to him which wasn't something a distinguished man did in that culture. When the son begins to speak, this young man does not even get his whole speech out. In verse 21, he confessed his sins, and after he'd done that, his father took over the conversation.

**How does the father respond to the son's confession and return?**

**The father in this parable is a stand-in for God the Father. What does this teach us about God's nature?**

All of a sudden the servants are sent scurrying when the father tells them to get his son a robe. That robe represents a place of honor. He also put a ring on his finger. The idea of the signet ring represents authority of the father. Next, he put sandals on his feet because a slave in that culture didn't have shoes. This son was so undone, he had walked home barefooted. Not only did the father clothe the son—he also had servants kill the fattened calf. This particular animal was specifically bred to be slaughtered at a time for significant celebration. To the father, the son's return called for a big party.

**What does this parable teach us about God's willingness to redeem those we might look at as unredeemable?**

The father did all of this because the prodigal son had come home. And this is the heart of God, because notice what he says, "For this, my son was dead and is alive again." "He was lost and is found." The prodigal never stopped being the father's son, even though he messed up, squandered a fortune, and even though he didn't want to be in the father's house. And that's the heart of God, my friends.

# THE OLDER BROTHER

In the previous personal study, we looked at the father's response to the prodigal coming home. Do you know what coming home is called in the Bible? It's called repentance. Repentance means to turn back. Repentance is not what saves you—Jesus saves you. But repentance is how we respond to Jesus and embrace what He's done. But not everyone was happy that the prodigal repented and returned home. In today's study, we'll take a look at how the older brother responded.

*Read Luke 15:25-32.*

**Why was the older brother unhappy about the party his father had thrown for his brother's homecoming?**

**Can you relate to the older brother? If so, how?**

# You Can Be Religious and Miss the Heart of God

This parable isn't just about the prodigal son. It's actually the parable of the two lost sons because we can also get lost when we stay, but we miss the heart of God. See, how Jesus turns it? Now this parable is about the Pharisees. He's like, "You know what your problem is? You're like the older brother." He's saying, "You have always stayed in the house of God. You have devoted your life to following the law, the Torah, you have done everything. You are the gold standard of how to be a religious person, but you miss the very heart of your Father."

**Glance back at verses 29-30. Why did the older brother feel he'd been slighted? Was he right to feel this way? Explain.**

The older brother felt that the father hadn't taken care of him. He felt that he'd been given the short end of the stick. This response revealed more about the older son than the father. We see the older brother's self-righteousness because we know that the father is good and loving. Yet the older brother feels that he hasn't been given enough. That is pride that we must avoid. Remember that Jesus was crucified, and he received it willingly. He embraced the short end of the stick for the sake of others and at great pain to Himself. A person with a self-righteousness attitude is always asserting his or her own rights.

**To some degree, we all struggle with pride and self-righteousness. In what areas do they tend to surface in your life?**

**How does this parable show that you can be "religious" and still miss the heart of God?**

Maybe you're like the prodigal who got his way, and you've squandered all sorts of things, my hope for you is that you would just come back and let the Father embrace you and celebrate you. Allow Him to forgive you.

Maybe you're realizing you're more like the older brother, you've stayed close, but you've missed the father's heart, my sincere hope for you is that you would repent of that because you don't know what happens with the older brother. He was mad at his father for being gracious and merciful and kind and generous. And if that's you, my prayer is that you turn back to Jesus. He will receive you.

# SESSION 6
# The Parable of the Talents

# GROUP STUDY

## Start

*Welcome everyone to session 6.*

The Bible has a lot to say about living with intentionality. We live in a fast-paced culture, and there are numerous ways to spend, invest, or waste our resources. Scripture makes it clear that we are not saved by our works—we are saved by grace through faith (Eph. 2:8-9). But for Christians, there's also an expectation to bear fruit for the kingdom of God. How we invest our time matters.

> **Who do you know who gets things done? What characteristics stand out about him or her?**
>
> **What are some ways your relationship with God influences how you spend your days?**

In this week's study, we'll be discussing the parable of the talents and what this story Jesus told means for modern-day believers.

*Pray and ask God to use your time together.*
*After praying, watch the video teaching.*

Video sessions available at lifeway.com/stories

# 𝔚𝔞𝔱𝔠𝔥

*Use the space below to take notes
while you watch video session 6.*

To access the teaching sessions,
use the instructions in the back
of your Bible study book.

# Discuss

The parable of the talents is a story about a manager who entrusted a different amount of money (talents were an ancient unit of measurement) to three servants. Through the story, we see God gives each one of us what He wants to give us. Our job is not to wish for a different set of gifts and talents, but rather to use what God has entrusted to us for His glory.

*Read Matthew 25:14-30 together.*

1.  All of us are saved by grace through faith in Christ (Eph. 2:8-9). However, why should the grace we've received lead us to pursue good works (Eph. 2:10)?

2.  This story is all about stewardship, which isn't a topic that is frequently discussed. How would you describe what it means to be a steward?

3.  Name a few things you are responsible for stewarding. Practically speaking, what would it look like to bear fruit for the kingdom of God as you steward these things?

4.  One of the lessons of this parable is that we should be aware of what God has given us and be seeking to use those resources to build His kingdom. What has God given you? How are you using it to bear fruit for His kingdom?

5.  How does stewarding your own talents free you from comparing your life or resources with other people's?

6.  Our lives matter, and what we do with our lives is important to the Lord. How do we make this attitude part of our mindset as followers of Jesus?

*Close your discussion with prayer. Remind those in your group to
complete the personal studies and Bible reading over the next week.*

# Reading Plan

*Over the next week, read the following passages to
further reflect upon the truths from this session.*

Psalm 1

John 15

Mark 11:12-14,20-25

Colossians 1:1-14

Galatians 5

**What do these Scriptures reveal about bearing
fruit for the kingdom of God?**

For the kingdom of heaven is like a man traveling to a far country, who called his own servants and delivered his goods to them. And to one he gave five talents, to another two, and to another one, to each according to his own ability; and immediately he went on a journey.

MATTHEW 25:14-15

# Personal Study 1

# THE PARABLE OF THE TALENTS

As we begin our last week of study, we'll take a look at the parable of the talents. Jesus' teaching makes it clear that our lives matter and how we spend our time here on earth matters to God.

*Read Matthew 25:14-30.*

**In your own words, describe the message for how we are to live as followers of Christ?**

**What evidence is there in this parable that God cares about how we spend our time and resources?**

**Name a few reasons why some people are more fruitful than others.**

## Talents Are For Investing

The master who's delivering these talents is extraordinarily wealthy because five talents would be the equivalent of 100 years' wages for the average person. This man is entrusting these servants with extraordinary amounts of money and gives to each one according to their abilities. He's not under any obligation to give any of the servants a certain amount, but he gives it to them and goes away. During his absence, one of the servants invested five of his talents and earned five more. Likewise, the man possessing two talents invested his talents and earned two more. But the third man found no joy in serving his master and, so he buried his only talent and got nothing in return. Because of the third man's unwillingness to maximize his only talent, the master took the servant's only talent and gave it to the man who had ten talents (v. 28).

**What do you think caused the third man to bury his only talent?**

**What are some ways we might "bury" the resources and talents God have given us?**

A close look at the parable reveals the third man's attitude toward his master impacted how he stewarded his resources. He had no love or reverence for his master, and so he was lazy with the resources his master entrusted to him. Like the servant, how we steward the resources that have been given to us reveals something about our regard for the giver. We are created for good works in Christ (Eph. 2:10). A failure to embrace this is a failure to be faithful.

**What gifts, talents, or resources has God given you?**

**How are you using the gifts, talents, and skills God has given you to honor Him and move His kingdom forward?**

If our faith is genuine, we will be good stewards of what God has entrusted to us as a way of showing our love to Him. This parable forces us to ask; do we want to be people who live with intentionality motivated by our love for God, or be condemned for our laziness?

# SHEEP AND GOATS

As we continue our study of the parable of the talents, we'll take a look at Jesus' teaching on the final judgment.

*Read Matthew 25:31-46.*

**How would you summarize Jesus' teaching in this passage?**

**Why don't more of us live with the awareness that our time will run out and there will be no further chances to commit our life to Christ? How does the finality of the passage make you feel?**

## Standing Before God

The previous passages we have studied have all been parables. While this passage sounds like a parable, it's more of a glimpse of what's to come in the final judgment. Jesus describes a time coming in the future when all people will stand before Him. The goats—who represent the lost who don't know Him—will be on His left (v. 33) while the sheep—who represent those who belong to God—will be on His right. Jesus will commend those on the right for providing food, water, shelter, clothing, and hospitality, and medical care for the "least of these." In this context, Jesus is referring to believers who came to the aid of their brothers and sisters in Christ (Matt. 25:40). That's not to say Christians aren't called to help unbelievers. Several places in the Bible command us to do so. But in this instance, Jesus is referring to serving other believers. Of course, these acts are not a means of salvation but rather evidence of a heart transformed by God

*Read the following passage.*

*For we must all appear before the judgment seat of Christ,
that each one may receive the things done in the body,
according to what he has done, whether good or bad.*
2 CORINTHIANS 5:10

**If you were to stand before Jesus today, are you confident you
would be on His right among His sheep? If not, what's holding you
back from giving your life to Jesus?**

**At this point in your life, how do you think Jesus would assess your
love and care for the least of these?**

**What steps is God leading you to take to be active in meeting needs
in your church and community?**

A time is coming when we will stand before Jesus face-to-face and give account
for the way we have lived. It would be insulting to the cross of Christ to ever
think we could pay Him back. But if we love Him, we will serve Him. Jesus has
given each one of us talents, resources, and everything we need for life and
godliness (2 Pet. 1:3). It's our responsibility to use all of it for His glory. If our
faith doesn't impact the way we live, there's good reason to question its authenticity (Jas. 2:14).

**How has this teaching personally challenged you?**

# WORKING UNTO THE LORD

The Bible makes it clear that for followers of Jesus, there's an expectation to bear fruit. But we must keep in mind, that no matter what we do, as believers, we work for God and not for men.

*Read the passage below.*

*And whatever you do, do it heartily, as to the Lord and not to men, knowing that from the Lord you will receive the reward of the inheritance; for you serve the Lord Christ.*
COLOSSIANS 3:23-24

**On a scale of 1 to 10, how would you rate your work ethic?**

**According to the passage above, what's the promise that comes along when working unto the Lord, rather than working for men?**

**How would your daily tasks be different if you approached them with the mindset that you were doing them for Jesus?**

One of the areas we get hung up on when we work hard and achieve success is we fall into the trap of thinking we're a self-made people. But in reality, there are no self-made people. We are a people created and maintained by God.

**What did Paul mean when he said we would receive an inheritance from the Lord?**

**Name a few ways God has gifted you with skills, talents, or life experience that has enriched your life or furthered your career.**

**How can you use these things for God's glory?**

**How can we do our normal job and regular routine, but as an offering to Jesus?**

Here's the thing. The very breath in your lungs is a gift. The fact that your heart is beating is a gift. The fact that you had enough food to make it this far is a gift. The fact that your body was able to utilize all these resources is a gift. Even the innate ability we have is a gift. None of us are self-made. We have been entrusted with great potential and the ability to use that potential. And Jesus asks us to use all these gifts to bear fruit for His kingdom. So, whatever those things are, we're supposed to do it heartily as onto the Lord.

# Stories Jesus Told
# LEADER GUIDE

# HOW TO USE THIS LEADER GUIDE

## Prepare to Lead

Before each session, go over the video teaching and read through the group discussion to prepare for the group meeting.

Familiarize yourself with the questions and begin thinking about how to best utilize these questions for the group you are leading. The following sections in the leader guide are given to help you facilitate the group well.

## Main Point

This section summarizes the big idea of each session. Use this section to help focus your preparation and leadership during the group session.

## Key Scriptures

The key passage of Scripture for the week is printed on the back-side of the leader guide for quick reference.

## Considerations

The purpose of leading a group is to bring God's Word to the people in the group. This section is designed to help you consider and wrestle with the ideas in each session and to suggest ways to apply those truths to your group.

## Pray

Use the prayer provided to close the leader guide or feel free to pray on your own.

# TIPS FOR LEADING A SMALL GROUP

## Prayerfully Prepare

Prepare for each group session with prayer. Ask the Holy Spirit to work through you and the discussion as you point to Jesus each week through God's Word.

REVIEW the personal studies and the group sessions ahead of time.

PRAY for each person in the group.

## Minimize Distractions

Do everything in your ability to help people focus on what's most important: connecting with God, with the Bible, and with one another.

Create a comfortable environment. If group members are uncomfortable, they'll be distracted and, therefore, not engaged in the group experience.

Take into consideration seating, temperature, lighting, refreshments, surrounding noise, and general cleanliness.

At best, thoughtfulness and hospitality show guests and group members they're welcome and valued in whatever environment you choose to gather. At worst, people may never notice your effort, but they're also not distracted.

## Include Others

Your goal is to foster a community in which people are welcome just as they are, but are encouraged to grow spiritually. Always be aware of opportunities to include anyone who visits the group and invite new people to join your group.

# Encourage Discussion

A good small-group experience has the following characteristics.

EVERYONE PARTICIPATES. Encourage everyone to ask questions, share responses, or read aloud.

NO ONE DOMINATES—NOT EVEN THE LEADER. Be sure your time speaking as a leader takes up less than half your time together as a group. Politely guide the discussion if anyone dominates.

NOBODY IS RUSHED THROUGH QUESTIONS. Don't feel that a moment of silence is a bad thing. People often need time to think about their responses to questions they've just heard or to gain courage to share what God is stirring in their hearts.

INPUT IS AFFIRMED AND FOLLOWED UP. Make sure you point out something true or helpful in a response. Don't just move on. Build community with follow-up questions, asking how other people have experienced similar things or how a truth has shaped their understanding of God and the Scripture you're studying. People are less likely to speak up if they fear that you don't actually want to hear their answers or that you're looking for only a certain answer.

GOD AND HIS Word ARE CENTRAL. Opinions and experiences can be helpful, but God has given us the truth. Trust Scripture to be the authority and God's Spirit to work in peoples' lives. You can't change anyone, but God can. Continually point people to the Word and to active steps of faith.

# Keep Connecting

Think of ways to connect with group members during the week. Participation during the group session always improves when members spend time connecting with one another outside the group sessions. The more people are comfortable with and involved in others' lives, the more they'll look forward to being together. When people move beyond being friendly to truly being friends who form a community, they come to each session eager to engage instead of merely attending.

# Session 1
# WHY PARABLES?

## Main Point

All believers want to hear God from God. The good news is we serve a God who communicates with His people. From the opening chapters of Genesis through the Book of Revelation, we see evidence that God is committed to speaking to those who want to hear. As modern-day believers, the primary way we hear from God is through His Word.

Jesus revealed that His reason for speaking in parables was two-fold. First, He spoke in parables to reveal truth to people who were willing to hear and believe. Also, to conceal truth from those who willingly reject it because of their calloused heart (13:15).

## Key Scriptures

See the passage on the back of this page.

## Considerations

Keep in mind that your group members will have various degrees of experience studying the Scripture. The idea is to reinforce the fact that the primary way God's people hear His voice and know His will is through the study of the Scriptures. Encourage each group member to set apart a time each day to read the Word. Remember, it's OK to start small—even a few minutes each day is a good place to start, especially if you are new to Bible study.

## Pray

*Ask God to give each person present an increased love and understanding of His Word. Pray that the Holy Spirit will teach them things they couldn't know apart from Him.*

# Why Jesus Taught in Parables

And the disciples came and said to Him, "Why do You speak to
them in parables?" He answered and said to them, "Because it
has been given to you to know the mysteries of the kingdom of
heaven, but to them it has not been given. For whoever has, to
him more will be given, and he will have abundance; but whoever
does not have, even what he has will be taken away from him.
Therefore I speak to them in parables, because seeing they do
not see, and hearing they do not hear, nor do they understand.
And in them the prophecy of Isaiah is fulfilled, which says:

Hearing you will hear and shall not understand,
And seeing you will see and not perceive;
For the hearts of this people have grown dull.
Their ears are hard of hearing,
And their eyes they have closed,
Lest they should see with their eyes and hear with their ears,
Lest they should understand with their hearts and turn,
So that I should heal them.'

But blessed are your eyes for they see, and your ears for
they hear; for assuredly, I say to you that many prophets
and righteous men desired to see what you see, and did not
see it, and to hear what you hear, and did not hear it."
MATTHEW 13:10-17

All these things Jesus spoke to the multitude in parables; and
without a parable He did not speak to them, that it might
be fulfilled which was spoken by the prophet, saying:
"I will open My mouth in parables;
I will utter things kept secret from the foundation of the world."
MATTHEW 13:34-35

## Session 2
# THE PARABLE OF THE SOILS

## Main Point

Jesus often used familiar concepts to explain unfamiliar spiritual truths. In the first century, Jesus ministered in an agrarian culture, so it's not surprising He used a farming example to illustrate a spiritual principle. In the parable of the sower, Jesus identified four potential types of soil that represent the human heart and He explained the parable in further detail. The four types of soils that Jesus mentions represent potential conditions of the human heart: a hard heart (v. 19), shallow heart (vv. 20-21) , worldly heart (v. 22), or an open heart that's receptive to God's truth (v. 23).

## Key Scriptures

See the passage on the back of this page.

## Considerations

Remember to emphasis the fact that at any given time all of us experience the four possible heart scenarios. We need to be intentional about accessing the spiritual condition of our heart. Good questions to ask are: Am I distracted? Too busy? Feeling hard-hearted? The goal for believers is to abide in Jesus, guard our hearts, and trust in Christ's power to bear fruit, because apart from Him we can do nothing.

## Pray

*Ask God to give each group member hearts that are open and receptive to His Word. Pray that they would abide in Jesus and bear fruit that brings glory to the Father. Ask God to give them wisdom to know how to guard their hearts.*

# Parable of the Sower

*Behold, a sower went out to sow. And as he sowed, some seed fell by the wayside; and the birds came and devoured them. Some fell on stony places, where they did not have much earth; and they immediately sprang up because they had no depth of earth. But when the sun was up they were scorched, and because they had no root they withered away. And some fell among thorns, and the thorns sprang up and choked them. But others fell on good ground and yielded a crop: some a hundredfold, some sixty, some thirty. He who has ears to hear, let him hear!*

*...*

*Therefore hear the parable of the sower: When anyone hears the word of the kingdom, and does not understand it, then the wicked one comes and snatches away what was sown in his heart. This is he who received seed by the wayside. But he who received the seed on stony places, this is he who hears the word and immediately receives it with joy; yet he has no root in himself, but endures only for a while. For when tribulation or persecution arises because of the word, immediately he stumbles. Now he who received seed among the thorns is he who hears the word, and the cares of this world and the deceitfulness of riches choke the word, and he becomes unfruitful. But he who received seed on the good ground is he who hears the word and understands it, who indeed bears fruit and produces: some a hundredfold, some sixty, some thirty.*

MATTHEW 13:19-23

## Session 3
# THE PARABLE OF LOST THINGS

## Main Point

God cares deeply for the lost. So much so, that Jesus' entire reason for coming was to seek the lost and reconcile them to the Father. The parables of the lost sheep and the lost coin reveals God's love for the lost. Why does He love the lost? Because He created them. Every single human being, no matter where they are in their spiritual journey, they've been created by God and they are His image-bearers. And all of us, at some point, were lost and disconnected from God. Jesus told the story to both the outcasts and the religious elite. No person or group was excluded from Jesus' circle.

## Key Scriptures

See the passage on the back of this page.

## Considerations

Keep in mind that there may be people in your group who don't yet know God. Emphasize the fact that God loves and accepts us the way we are, but He loves us too much to leave us in our sin. Spend time talking about the importance of repentance. Pastor Daniel said, "Repentance is a change of mind that leads to a change of heart, which leads to a change of direction." Stress the point that we never outgrow our need for repentance—it should be a daily spiritual discipline for believers.

## Pray

*Ask God to reveal people who need to hear the gospel and respond to Christ's salvation. Pray for opportunities to share why your life is different since you belong to Jesus.*

# Parable of the Lost Sheep

*What man of you, having a hundred sheep, if he loses one of them, does not leave the ninety-nine in the wilderness, and go after the one which is lost until he finds it? And when he has found it, he lays it on his shoulders, rejoicing. And when he comes home, he calls together his friends and neighbors, saying to them, "Rejoice with me, for I have found my sheep which was lost!"I say to you that likewise there will be more joy in heaven over one sinner who repents than over ninety-nine just persons who need no repentance.*
LUKE 15:4-7

# Parable of the Lost Coin

*Or what woman, having ten silver coins, if she loses one coin, does not light a lamp, sweep the house, and search carefully until she finds it? And when she has found it, she calls her friends and neighbors together, saying, "Rejoice with me, for I have found the piece which I lost!" Likewise, I say to you, there is joy in the presence of the angels of God over one sinner who repents."*
LUKE 15:8-10

# Session 4
# THE PARABLE OF
# THE WHEAT AND WEEDS

## Main Point

When Jesus' disciples approached Him asking questions about this parable, He explained that the wheat and weeds represent good and evil in the world. Many Jews who'd been waiting for the coming of the Messiah anticipated that when He came, He would immediately eradicate evil from the world—but that wasn't God's plan. Some were confused and questioned Jesus' authority. But in this parable, Jesus demonstrated He was not the source of evil. The entire world belongs to God, the enemy has no right to bring evil into the world, and the Son of God will assert His authority over the world at the time of judgment. But for now, there's a combination of both good and evil in the world.

## Key Scriptures

See the passage on the back of this page.

## Considerations

Keep in mind you might have people in your group who have had unfortunate experiences at church. Be sure to show sensitivity to their situation while stressing that even though church isn't perfect, we are still called to be active members of biblical community. It is our role to abide in Christ and stay in Christian fellowship. We should never be ignorant of the enemy's plan to wreak havoc. But if we were to drop out of church life we'd be allowing the enemy to steal the community Jesus desires for us to have in Him.

## Pray

*Ask God to increase our wisdom and give us discernment in our relationships. Pray each group member will abide in Christ and find an active role in biblical community.*

# The Parable of the Wheat and the Weeds

*The kingdom of heaven is like a man who sowed good seed in his field; but while men slept, his enemy came and sowed tares among the wheat and went his way. But when the grain had sprouted and produced a crop, then the tares also appeared. So the servants of the owner came and said to him, "Sir, did you not sow good seed in your field? How then does it have tares?" He said to them, "An enemy has done this." The servants said to him, "Do you want us then to go and gather them up?" But he said, "No, lest while you gather up the tares you also uproot the wheat with them. Let both grow together until the harvest, and at the time of harvest I will say to the reapers, 'First gather together the tares and bind them in bundles to burn them, but gather the wheat into my barn.'"*

MATTHEW 13:24-30

## Session 5
# THE PARABLE OF THE PRODGIAL SON

## Main Point

The story of the prodigal son reveals God's heart for the lost. But this parable isn't just about the prodigal son. It's actually the parable of the two lost sons because we can also get lost when we stray, but we miss the heart of God. Regardless of how we stray, the Father waits with His eyes on the horizon for our return. If we'll repent and come home to Him, God stands ready waiting to forgive and embrace us.

## Key Scriptures

See the passage on the back of this page.

## Considerations

Remember, there's likely people in your group who have prodigals in their life. Stress the fact that God's love is stronger than any sin we can commit and no one is beyond His reach. Spend time talking about what it means to repent and why repentance should be a daily spiritual discipline in the life of the believer.

## Pray

*Ask God to bring the prodigals you know to the foot of the cross. Pray that each group member would recognize their tendency to either be a prodigal or the older brother. Ask that each person present would be quick to repent and embrace God's forgiveness.*

# Parable of the Prodigal Son

A certain man had two sons. And the younger of them said to his father, "Father, give me the portion of goods that falls to me." So he divided to them his livelihood. And not many days after, the younger son gathered all together, journeyed to a far country, and there wasted his possessions with prodigal living. But when he had spent all, there arose a severe famine in that land, and he began to be in want. Then he went and joined himself to a citizen of that country, and he sent him into his fields to feed swine. And he would gladly have filled his stomach with the pods that the swine ate, and no one gave him anything. But when he came to himself, he said, "How many of my father's hired servants have bread enough and to spare, and I perish with hunger! I will arise and go to my father, and will say to him, 'Father, I have sinned against heaven and before you, and I am no longer worthy to be called your son. Make me like one of your hired servants.'" And he arose and came to his father. But when he was still a great way off, his father saw him and had compassion, and ran and fell on his neck and kissed him. And the son said to him, "Father, I have sinned against heaven and in your sight, and am no longer worthy to be called your son." But the father said to his servants, "Bring out the best robe and put it on him, and put a ring on his hand and sandals on his feet. And bring the fatted calf here and kill it, and let us eat and be merry; for this my son was dead and is alive again; he was lost and is found." And they began to be merry. Now his older son was in the field. And as he came and drew near to the house, he heard music and dancing. So he called one of the servants and asked what these things meant. And he said to him, "Your brother has come, and because he has received him safe and sound, your father has killed the fatted calf." But he was angry and would not go in. Therefore his father came out and pleaded with him. So he answered and said to his father, "Lo, these many years I have been serving you; I never transgressed your commandment at any time; and yet you never gave me a young goat, that I might make merry with my friends. But as soon as this son of yours came, who has devoured your livelihood with harlots, you killed the fatted calf for him." And he said to him, "Son, you are always with me, and all that I have is yours. It was right that we should make merry and be glad, for your brother was dead and is alive again, and was lost and is found."

LUKE 15:11-32

# Session 6
# THE PARABLE OF THE TALENTS

## Main Point

The parable of the talents reveals that God cares about how we invest our lives, and for believers, there is an expectation of fruitfulness. Keep in mind, our salvation is by grace through faith, and it can't be earned by works (Eph. 2:8-9). However, if our faith is genuine, we will be good stewards of what God has entrusted to us as a way of showing our love to Him. This parable forces us to ask; do we want to be people who live with intentionality motivated by our love for God, or be condemned for our laziness?

## Key Scriptures

See the passage on the back of this page.

## Considerations

A time is coming when we will stand before Jesus face-to-face and give account for the way we have lived. It would be insulting to the cross of Christ to ever think we could pay Him back. But if we love Him, we will serve Him. Jesus has given each one of us talents, resources, and everything we need for life and godliness (2 Pet. 1:3). It's our responsibility to use all of it for His glory. If our faith doesn't impact the way we live, there's good reason to question its authenticity (Jas. 2:14).

## Pray

*Ask God to empower each group member to maximize their talents for the kingdom of God. Pray each person will have a strong sense of the fact that they are saved by grace through faith and that they live their lives in gratitude.*

# Parable of the Talents

*For the kingdom of heaven is like a man traveling to a far country, who called his own servants and delivered his goods to them. And to one he gave five talents, to another two, and to another one, to each according to his own ability; and immediately he went on a journey. Then he who had received the five talents went and traded with them, and made another five talents. And likewise he who had received two gained two more also. But he who had received one went and dug in the ground, and hid his lord's money. After a long time the lord of those servants came and settled accounts with them. So he who had received five talents came and brought five other talents, saying, "Lord, you delivered to me five talents; look, I have gained five more talents besides them." His lord said to him, "Well done, good and faithful servant; you were faithful over a few things, I will make you ruler over many things. Enter into the joy of your lord." He also who had received two talents came and said, "Lord, you delivered to me two talents; look, I have gained two more talents besides them." His lord said to him, "Well done, good and faithful servant; you have been faithful over a few things, I will make you ruler over many things. Enter into the joy of your lord." Then he who had received the one talent came and said, "Lord, I knew you to be a hard man, reaping where you have not sown, and gathering where you have not scattered seed. And I was afraid, and went and hid your talent in the ground. Look, there you have what is yours." But his lord answered and said to him, "You wicked and lazy servant, you knew that I reap where I have not sown, and gather where I have not scattered seed. So you ought to have deposited my money with the bankers, and at my coming I would have received back my own with interest. So take the talent from him, and give it to him who has ten talents. For to everyone who has, more will be given, and he will have abundance; but from him who does not have, even what he has will be taken away. And cast the unprofitable servant into the outer darkness. There will be weeping and gnashing of teeth."*
MATTHEW 25:14-30

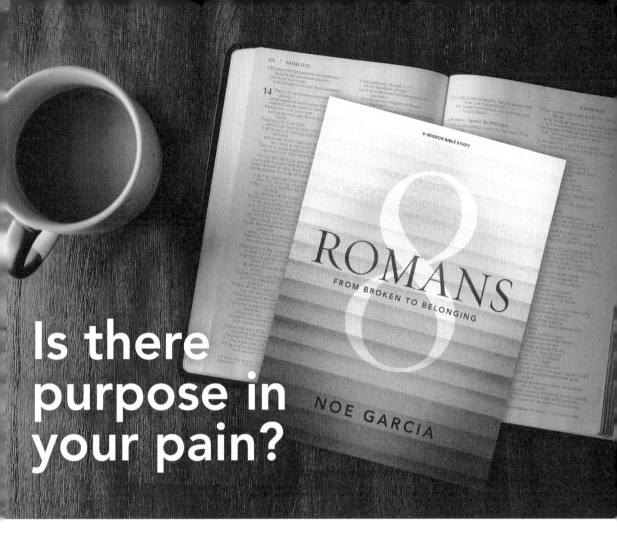

# Is there purpose in your pain?

Do things like depression, anxiety, hurting relationships, and unmet expectations cause you to question God? Have you ever thought your life was beyond repair or wondered if God could use your brokenness for good?

In this new eight-session Bible study, Noe Garcia takes participants on a journey through Romans 8 while sharing his personal experiences of abuse, depression, and overwhelming hopelessness.

He reveals how God redeemed, repaired, and restored him, and he'll help you understand Christ's transformative power to repurpose hurt and brokenness for your good and His glory.

---

Access to session videos is included with the purchase of the Bible Study Book, and videos are also available through Lifeway on Demand.

# How to read your Bible better and more often

Reading the Bible is a fundamental part of Christianity. But reading it consistently and purposely can be difficult. The *Foundations* family makes it much easier. Each resource provides a one-year, five-days-per-week reading plan, which helps you build the habit of daily study but offers flexibility so you don't get behind. And the HEAR journaling method leads you to highlight, explain, apply, and respond, so you get even more out of your time in God's Word.

Journeys
are navigated
not by waves but by

# STARS

It's tempting to measure your success as a Christian by the sins you avoid, your good deeds, or what your friends are doing. This method quickly drifts into wave after wave of comparison or even legalism. But there is a healthy way to check the progress of your spiritual journey. This new Bible study discusses six biblical traits that are commonly seen in the lives of growing disciples. As you follow these markers like navigational stars, your faith can advance in the way God intended.

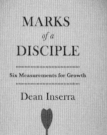

MARKS
*of a*
DISCIPLE

Six Measurements for Growth

Dean Inserra

# The timeless parables of Jesus.

Many authors use parables to illustrate truth. But when those stories are being told by the Son of God, we should listen even more carefully. Though Jesus shared these parables many centuries ago, they still speak to us today.

*Stories Jesus Told* is your opportunity to sit at the feet of the Master and listen. You may have heard some of His parables before, but there is always something new to learn from Jesus. And author Daniel Fusco has a few things to say as well. His insights and stories will help you examine your own heart, remember God's love for the lost, celebrate His mercy, connect what you believe to what you do, and more.

- Gain a clearer understanding of why Jesus taught the way He did.
- See Jesus' heart and compassion through some of the most memorable and best-loved teaching in Scripture.
- Peel back the layers of your own heart to discover what's truly important to you.

## ADDITIONAL RESOURCES

**VIDEO CONTENT**
Streamable session videos featuring Daniel Fusco are included with the purchase price of this book. Look for your access code on the attached insert.

**eBOOK**
The eBook includes the content of this printed book but offers the convenience and flexibility that comes with mobile technology.

**DVD SET**
Recommended for individuals or groups that may want to redo the study again at a later date.

**TEEN BIBLE STUDY BOOK**

**More resources can be found online at lifeway.com/storiesjesustold**

*Price and availability subject to change without notice.*